AFRICA'S ANIMALS

A Ridge Press Book/Doubleday/New York

publisher: JERRY MASON
editor: ADOLPH SUEHSDORF
art director: ALBERT SQUILLACE
associate editors: MOIRA DUGGAN, FRANCES FOLEY
art associates: ALLAN MOGEL, DAVID NAMIAS
art production: DORIS MULLANE

Photo credits:

MARVIN NEWMAN: Pages 4-5, 6-7, 8-9, 10-11, 12-13,
14-15, 16-17, 18-19, 20-21, 22-23, 27, 32 top, 33, 35,
38, 40-41, 46-47, 48-49, 50-51, 52-53, 54-55, 56-57,
58-59, 64-65, 66-67, 68, 70-71, 72-73, 74-75, 76-77,
78-79, 80.

ELIOT ELISOFON: Pages 24-25, 26, 28-29, 30-31, 32
bottom, 34, 36-37, 39, 42-43, 44-45, 60-61, 62-63, 69.

Africa's Animals is a Ridge Press / ABC book
Published by Doubleday & Co.

Printed in the United States of America by Western
Printing and Lithographing Company, Inc.

Copyright © 1967 by Ridge Press, Inc. and the
American Broadcasting Companies, Inc.

Library of Congress Catalog Card Number 67-21145

Contents

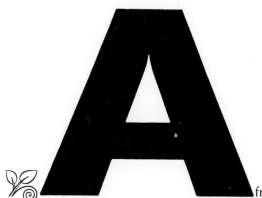

frica is a treasure land. There are dia-
monds in the earth, spaces that stretch forever, mountains lost in clouds, forests filled with life and beauty. Of all
Africa's treasures, one of the greatest is its animals. There are hundreds of species of mammals and birds, grazers and
browsers, predators and scavengers, tree climbers and amphibians. And all of them, great and small, are busy about
the business of surviving. The governments of Africa, too, are busy trying to preserve their irreplaceable treasure
of wildlife. Many of the countries are newly established, many of their leaders are new to the ways of governing, and
hardly any of them is rich enough to do the job as well as it would like. But they are trying. There are already
fifteen large game sanctuaries in six African countries, and there will surely be more. Luckily for the animals, they
attract tourists, and the money the tourists spend helps to pay the cost of maintaining the parks and reserves.
The new governments regulate legal hunting more carefully than ever before, and penalize poachers—illegal
hunters—more highly than ever. Africans are being trained as park administrators who use both scientific knowledge
and mercy in controlling and preserving the game levels. They face enormous problems: moving tribes to make
room for animals; dealing with poachers, some of whom are guilty of no more than hunger. And there is the problem
of keeping the animals within the boundaries of a sanctuary. How do you fence in an area of 11,000 square miles?
Scientists, too, must discover secrets of ecology they have not yet dreamed of—how the life of one species affects
the lives of the others and the food supply of all. Then there is man, with his ever-growing civilization. The animals
of the African wild are in danger, but man has at least awakened to the need to save them. The color pictures
in this book, by photographers Marvin Newman and Eliot Elisofon, show twenty-two of the best-known species of
Africa's animals living in their natural habitats. They were taken as part of the American Broadcasting Company's Africa,
an effort to convey through television a true and comprehensive picture of the various aspects of life in the countries
of Africa. As much as pictures can, they make it possible to see Africa's animals as they really are: free and
awe-inspiring—the living treasure of the African continent.

Lions are Africa's most powerful predators. Heroic size, strength, and speed enable them to conquer even such mighty animals as the rhino and the Cape buffalo, to overtake sprinters as fast as the antelopes. Their only deadly enemy is man. Lions live on grassy plains in groups called "prides," which may number from five to fifteen, or as many as forty. Prides often occupy one tract of land and will drive off any strange lions that intrude. Within the pride, members are loyal and affectionate, nuzzling and licking each other when they meet. Cubs are born in litters of two or three, and by two years of age only the females are still with the pride. A grown lion may measure 9 feet from nose to tail and weigh about 400 pounds. Females run a foot shorter and 100 pounds lighter. The mane is a male characteristic, but it varies with the individual: some have a great mantle, others a neck ruff, and some have no mane at all.

Lions when fed and content are the picture of relaxation. Let others graze and hunt in the heat of the day; the lion prefers to loll those hours away in tall grass or the shade of a tree. But a hungry lion is a different story. Prodded by hunger, it becomes active, bold, determined, and very much the King of Beasts. Lions will eat almost anything, but prefer animals, like the zebra and wildebeest, that are big enough to feed the pride. Hunting is done at night, and the lioness usually makes the kill, although males will help bring down large animals, like the giraffe and the Cape buffalo. Often the male circles upwind of the prey and then, with a mighty roar, stampedes it into the path of a waiting female. Over a short distance, she can run at a speed of 35 miles per hour, fast enough to keep up with all but the swiftest grazing game. The kill is made by gripping the prey's throat in a suffocating bite, or by leaping onto its back and clawing its muzzle to turn the head, so that the animal stumbles and falls. Young lions go through a long and arduous training period in learning to hunt. As cubs they are taught to attack game caught and held for them by the lioness. In the first year of life the cubs do plenty of playful mauling and wrestling and learn to use their fangs and claws. At eighteen months they have the size and weight to try bringing down game in the field. It is often a painful lesson, as the biting, kicking victims throw off the awkward student. In time, however, the young lion learns to coordinate his strength, weight, and weapons. When this time comes, nothing in his domain can stand up to him. From then on, he is monarch of all he surveys.

The silent, solitary leopard is Africa's most clever hunter, apart from man. It is smaller than the lion, but stronger for its weight. It is also an excellent tree-climber and swimmer, which the lion is not. The leopard prefers the heavy brush and thick cover of the forest, and when not hunting it likes to doze the afternoon away on the limb of a tree. It takes its prey from ambush and counts on the element of surprise. Impalas are its favorite meat, though an antelope of any species, not more than twice the cat's weight, will do. In fact, the leopard is not a very choosy eater. Let a jackal, bush pig, warthog, baboon, guinea fowl, or wild dog come near its lair when the leopard is hungry and the chase is on. Down from his lair he glides and into cover. A patient, stealthy stalk, and the distance between hunter and prey grows short. A final crouch to gather his muscles and the leopard springs. The prey, surprised, will dash for freedom, but unless it is very, very lucky, the leopard is soon upon it. The kill is quick, and then—if the prey is large—the leopard pulls it up into a tree to keep it from lions and hyenas. The cat may feed on this meal for two or three days. A leopard's hunting ground is large but well-defined, and unless the cat is disturbed it will stay there for years, moving every few days to a different vantage point.

Although not a sociable animal, the leopard will often remain in an area that is well-settled, living off domestic rather than wild animals. Unless bothered, it lives quietly and alone and avoids man. Even so, it is an animal to be feared. A fine leopard may be 7 feet long and weigh 140 pounds. The male stays with its mate for only a short time, going off before the litter of two or three cubs is born. A typical day in the life of a grown leopard is spent basking in the morning, napping in the afternoon, and hunting all night. His most troublesome neighbors are the baboons and monkeys. When these forest-dwellers catch sight of their great natural enemy, they scramble through the treetops after it, chattering and screaming warnings of its presence. Naturalists point out that in areas where leopards have been hunted out of existence, there is a serious increase of agricultural pests such as monkeys. Still, these mighty hunters are widely hunted. They are one of the Big Five trophies and licenses to shoot them have plenty of takers, even though the permits are expensive and only a limited number are issued each year. Yet only a fraction of the leopards killed go to the legal hunters. Poachers, spurred by the high prices offered for the marvelously spotted pelts, take all the leopards they can get. For the time being, man can indulge himself in leopard-skin coats and rugs. But soon he will have to do without them.

Cheetah, found in Asia as well as Africa, is a hunter built for running down its prey. The body is streamlined, the legs long, the muscles bunched at the shoulders and hindquarters. Cheetah is the fastest of all animals. From a standing start it can reach 45 mph in two seconds, and keep a pace of 60 to 70 mph for well over 100 yards. Given a good jump, it can usually run down a gazelle, its favorite meat. It may hunt in tandem with another, but mostly it is a "loner." In many ways it is unlike the other cat species. It relies on the chase rather than surprise to take its prey. It hunts by day rather than night. And, like members of the dog family, it cannot pull in its claws. There is something special about sighting a cheetah in the open. They are sparsely distributed and easily mistaken for leopards. The handsome coat is a pale yellow with dark brown spots. A ruff that rises along the back of the neck adds a dash of menace to the cat's otherwise mild mien. For all of its dangerous assets, the cheetah actually has an easy-going nature. Many have been turned into affectionate pets that can miaow as contentedly as any old tabby.

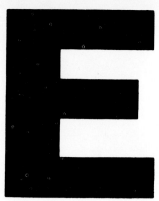

Elephants are gigantic, majestic, and inspiring to behold. A mature bull measures nearly 11 feet at the shoulder and weighs up to seven tons. His tusks, longer and heavier than the Indian elephant's, may weigh 100 pounds each. (The record length for one tusk, measured along the curve, is 11½ feet; record weight: 235 pounds.) To fuel its vast bulk, the elephant eats 300 to 400 pounds of vegetation—leaves, bark, roots, bamboo and papyrus, grass and seed pods—every day. The animals knock over large trees with trunk or forehead to get at roots and foliage. To topple a really big one, several elephants will work together. Tusks are used as levers in digging and uprooting. In a day a herd of elephants feeds for sixteen hours and may range as far as thirty miles in search of food and water. The average pace is 5 mph, but this can be doubled with a long, shuffling stride when pressed. In their migrations the herds habitually use established elephant trails. It is said that many of Africa's first motor roads simply followed these trails because of the animals' unerring instinct for finding the easiest way over hilly terrain. Elephants also create water holes for other animals by the seepage of water into the footprints they make in sandy river beds. When rivers disappear in the dry season, elephants will dig little wells with their trunks, at which herd members line up in order of seniority to come and drink.

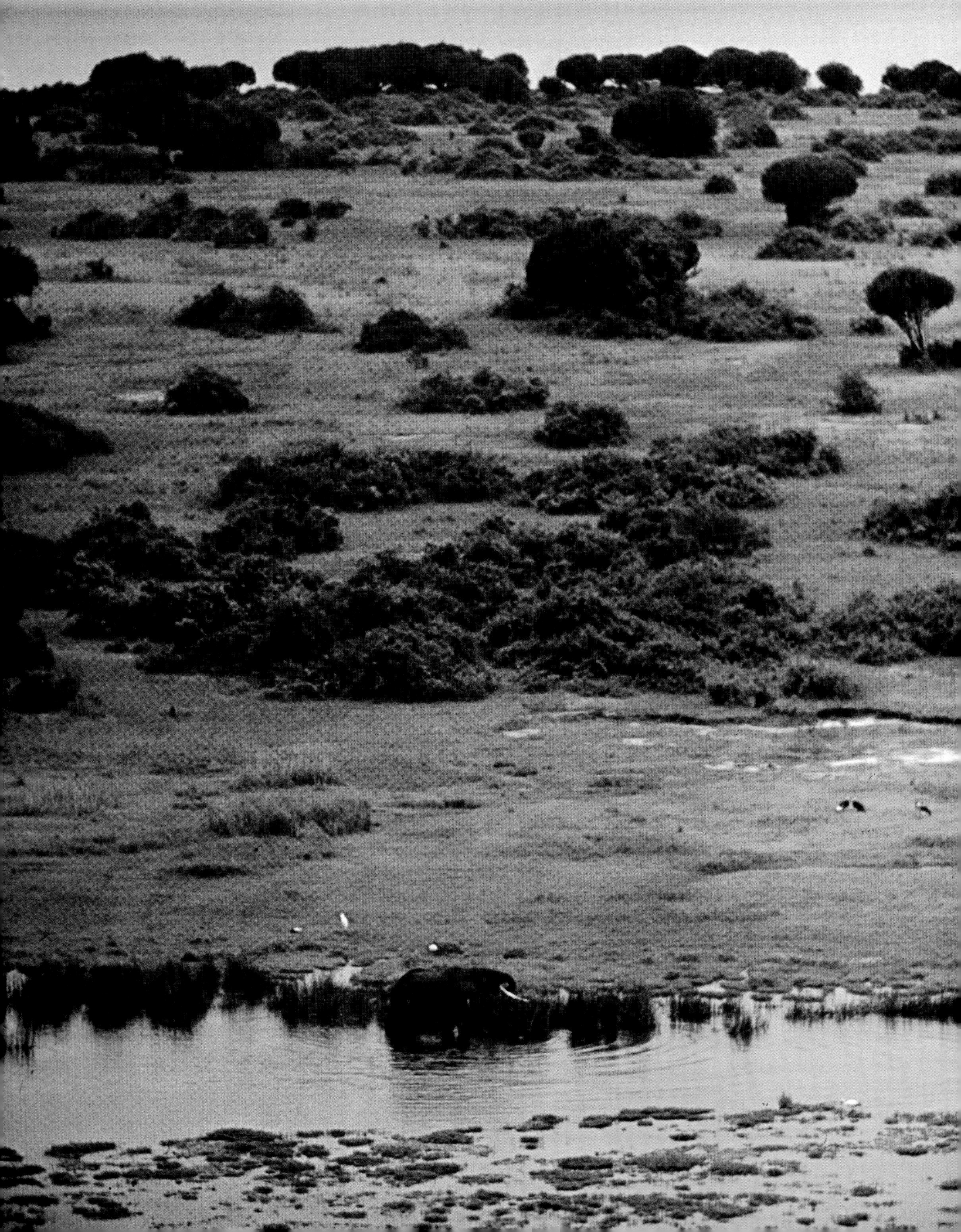

Africa has two races of elephants: the great bush race that ranges the savannas of the East and South, and the smaller forest elephant that inhabits the jungles of West Africa and the Congo. Both are bigger than the Indian species, and—unlike the Asian elephants—they are not easily trained as beasts of burden. Elephants band together in family groups of perhaps fifteen cows and calves and several young bulls. Family groups sometimes combine to form companies numbering up to two hundred. Old bulls travel alone, joining the band for bathing and drinking, but otherwise preferring a placid existence away from the noisy and temperamental cows and calves. An elephant cow may have a dozen young over her lifetime. Her calves weigh about 200 pounds at birth and stay with her for two years. The cows are careful, affectionate mothers. They bathe their young, protect them, and, when they are disobedient, spank them with an uprooted bush. Life for the elephant herds is more or less tranquil. No longer are incredible numbers of elephants slaughtered for their ivory tusks alone. In many of the African game parks they have become so numerous that it is necessary to keep the numbers down by control shooting. But the great elephants need more than protection. They need the space to range freely. In time to come, Africa may not have the land to spare.

R

hinoceros have the reputation of being very easily angered, and visitors to the animal parks give them a very wide berth. The rhino, it is true, seems to live by a simple rule of survival: When in doubt, charge! The least annoyance brings the rhino running with a swift, bouncing gait, snorting all the while. If really provoked, it can charge at 30 miles an hour. There are reasons why the rhino behaves as it does. Its vision is very poor, giving it little chance to size up a situation of possible danger. Also, it is a more or less solitary beast, and has none of the protection shared by animals in a herd. Man hunts the rhino for its horns. Poachers kill great numbers of the animals and sell the horns at a high price to dealers in medicinals and "love potions." The more placid "white" rhino, a grazer unlike the leaf-eating black species, may soon be extinct. Rhino's future is in doubt. It depends on protection by humans and by the qualities that have helped it survive until now: its inch-thick hide, its speed and agility, and its sheer enormity.

Cape buffalo lounging on the African plain are as awesome to see as the thunderheads that pile up in the African sky. And, like those clouds that sometimes break in wild storms, the buffalo, too, hold the promise of great destructiveness. A mature bull may weigh a ton, stand 5 feet at the shoulder, and carry horns measuring more than 4 feet at the outside curves. The appearance is cow-like; the personality is not. Buffalo have keen senses of sight, smell, and hearing. They are inquisitive. Hunters would even call them crafty. Goaded by a wound or a challenge, this normally placid animal may drive native hunters into brush where their bows and arrows are useless, or charge a rifleman at 35 mph. Yet, when undisturbed, it is content to graze in water-fed environments— river valleys, reedy swamps, and lush forests; to sleep off the heat of the day in cool, shady spots; to spend the night bathing and ruminating. Thanks to careful preservation, the herds are holding their own. Man hunts the African buffalo mainly for its magnificent horns.

H

ippopotamus, meaning "water horse," was the Greeks' word for it. This sociable beast spends the day submerged in rivers and lakes, strolling along the bottom, cavorting, quarreling, courting, coming up to breathe, and in general fulfilling its natural function as bulldozer of the waterways. Towards evening the ponderous hippo pulls itself out of the water on stumpy legs to graze its daily 50 pounds of grass on firm ground. Hippos mate, give birth, and nurse their young in the water. One of the few things that rouses a hippo to anger is a threat to its calf. Hippos are one of the most fascinating species to watch. Being "contact" animals, they require the closeness and physical contact of group living. It is evident in their water play, and in their way of flopping down in friendly heaps to drowse. As swimmers, they are not the least bit clumsy, despite the 4,000 pounds of rotundity a large bull may carry. When the gigantic mouth is agape, as it often is, two great ivory tusks are seen, curving up at the corners of the lower jaw. In fights between bulls, the tusks are used as slashing weapons. Otherwise they are to the hippo's misfortune, since the soft, grainless quality of the ivory is much prized by man. Still, there is less problem with protecting hippos than controlling them. Where they survive they tend to multiply fast and to overgraze the land. When this happens, the "water horses" can turn a lush, green area into one that is almost completely bare of vegetation.

Greatest leaper in Africa is the impala, a graceful antelope that can bound across the plain in great 20-foot jumps. Impalas are a familiar sight in Africa, their sleek, well-formed bodies and lyre-shaped horns always a thrilling sight, especially when the herd takes flight in alarm. The lion, cheetah, wild dog, and leopard are their enemies but, unless taken by surprise, the impala can usually outrun any pursuer. In flight, an impala's black and white tail becomes a flag marking the way of escape for those at the rear of the herd. Alert impalas also signal danger with a high, "sneezing" snort.

In courting season the gentle impalas present another picture. Desperate fights break out among the rams, with the
losers going off to form bands of their own. Impalas move
across the grasslands in large herds of from ten to fifty,
often mingled with other animals such as the giraffe and
wildebeest. They stay near water and drink regularly, in
the morning, mid-day, and evening. The lion and the
leopard know that water holes are good places to stalk
impala. As evening falls on the plain, many a big cat is
dining on impala. Happily, the lovely animals are plentiful.

Thomson's gazelles, the bright little creatures streaming across the top of these pages, are everybody's favorite dish. Jackals prey on the newborn. Leopard, cheetah, and wild dog hunt the adults. And hunters on safari find Tommies a tasty addition to the stewpot. They are among the smaller of the grazing antelope species, measuring no more than 2 feet at the shoulder and weighing at most 60 pounds. They are mild-mannered and naturally tame, although a little Tommy ram is not afraid to buck a jackal to protect a fawn. Tommies are noted for "stotting" when alarmed. This is a series of stiff-legged jumps, made with head and tail erect. Fortunately for everyone, Thomson's gazelles are in good supply.

Hartebeest (left) and its subspecies, topi (right), are two of the antelopes that grace the plain. Lookalikes in many ways, hartebeest's horns join at the base, topi's do not.

Wildebeest's hindquarters are sleek and well-muscled and betray its membership in the graceful antelope family. Beyond this, observers find the wildebeest a homely beast, indeed. Below its humped shoulders, it carries a long-muzzled head with smallish horns and a stingy beard. It looks a bit front-heavy, as though it might topple over on its face. But no need to pity the wildebeest! This grass-eater is faster at the gallop than a racehorse, and its dumb expression belies a frolicsome nature. It is alert and skittish, especially at water holes, though it also has a curiosity that sometimes leads it into

danger and, alas, into the teeth of a lion. Yet it defends itself so courageously that predators have a tough time with all but weaklings and straggling youngsters. During the summer dry season, visitors to the Serengeti Park in Tanzania witness an unforgettable sight: an endless file of wildebeest and zebra migrating to green grass and water hundreds of miles away. In the past, great numbers of this species (named gnu by the Hottentots and wildebeest by the Dutch) were killed by man for the most shameful of reasons: to use their tails as flyswatters.

Z

ebras, the wild horses of Africa, are one of the most decorative elements in the landscape. Their black and white stripes are beautifully patterned, their brush-like manes have a well-groomed look, and they move with an air of roly-poly jauntiness. All this makes it easy to forgive the zebra's less lovable qualities. It is a noisy, nervous, and ill-mannered beast, especially at water holes, where it does plenty of nipping and kicking. Zebras are grazers, and with their cronies, the wildebeest, they will migrate long distances in dry season to reach grass and water. They occur in many areas of Africa: the wide-striped Burchell's zebra in herds of up to twenty, and the narrow-striped Grévy's zebra, of more northerly habitats, in herds of up to thirty. Their camouflage is most effective at dusk, the time when lions are on the prowl for meat. Zebras are ever alert against this enemy, entering high grass only with reluctance. Many a meeting between the two ends in a stand-off, for the lion will not usually pounce unless it has stalked to within 40 yards of a thoroughly unsuspecting prey. When zebras sense a stalking lion, they bolt away just out of range, then turn to stare at the marauder, aware that the promise of their powerful hooves and vicious teeth will keep the lion off. Not so with man. Rifle power is something the zebra has learned to fear. At the sound of a shot a herd takes off and gallops for miles. Even so, many are shot, sometimes just for their handsome hides.

Giraffe have a graceful, dreamlike gallop that is one of Africa's memorable sights. This is the tallest animal on earth, growing to between 18 and 19 feet. It feeds on the leaves of trees, its long neck reaching among the branches, its prehensile tongue drawing in the tender leaves and shoots it savors. Beyond this adaptation for browsing, the animal's physique has few assets. Only by splaying its front legs wide can it lower its head far enough to drink, and in this awkward position, it is vulnerable to attack. The mosaic camouflage of its coat works only in leafy shade; seen in the open, the coat becomes quite eye-catching. In an environment where predators abound, the giraffe would rather run from danger. Yet, if it must, it will defend itself from attack, flailing with its large, sharp hooves. Left in peace, giraffes are gentle creatures. The fond nuzzling between male and female during courtship is much in character. Of this animal, the Danish writer Isak Dinesen, who lived many years in Africa, said: "A giraffe is so much a lady that one refrains from thinking of her legs, but remembers her as floating over the plains in long garbs, draperies of morning mist and mirage."

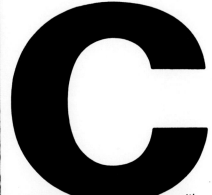

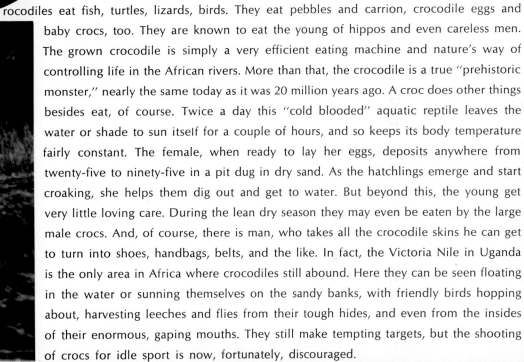

C

rocodiles eat fish, turtles, lizards, birds. They eat pebbles and carrion, crocodile eggs and baby crocs, too. They are known to eat the young of hippos and even careless men. The grown crocodile is simply a very efficient eating machine and nature's way of controlling life in the African rivers. More than that, the crocodile is a true "prehistoric monster," nearly the same today as it was 20 million years ago. A croc does other things besides eat, of course. Twice a day this "cold blooded" aquatic reptile leaves the water or shade to sun itself for a couple of hours, and so keeps its body temperature fairly constant. The female, when ready to lay her eggs, deposits anywhere from twenty-five to ninety-five in a pit dug in dry sand. As the hatchlings emerge and start croaking, she helps them dig out and get to water. But beyond this, the young get very little loving care. During the lean dry season they may even be eaten by the large male crocs. And, of course, there is man, who takes all the crocodile skins he can get to turn into shoes, handbags, belts, and the like. In fact, the Victoria Nile in Uganda is the only area in Africa where crocodiles still abound. Here they can be seen floating in the water or sunning themselves on the sandy banks, with friendly birds hopping about, harvesting leeches and flies from their tough hides, and even from the insides of their enormous, gaping mouths. They still make tempting targets, but the shooting of crocs for idle sport is now, fortunately, discouraged.

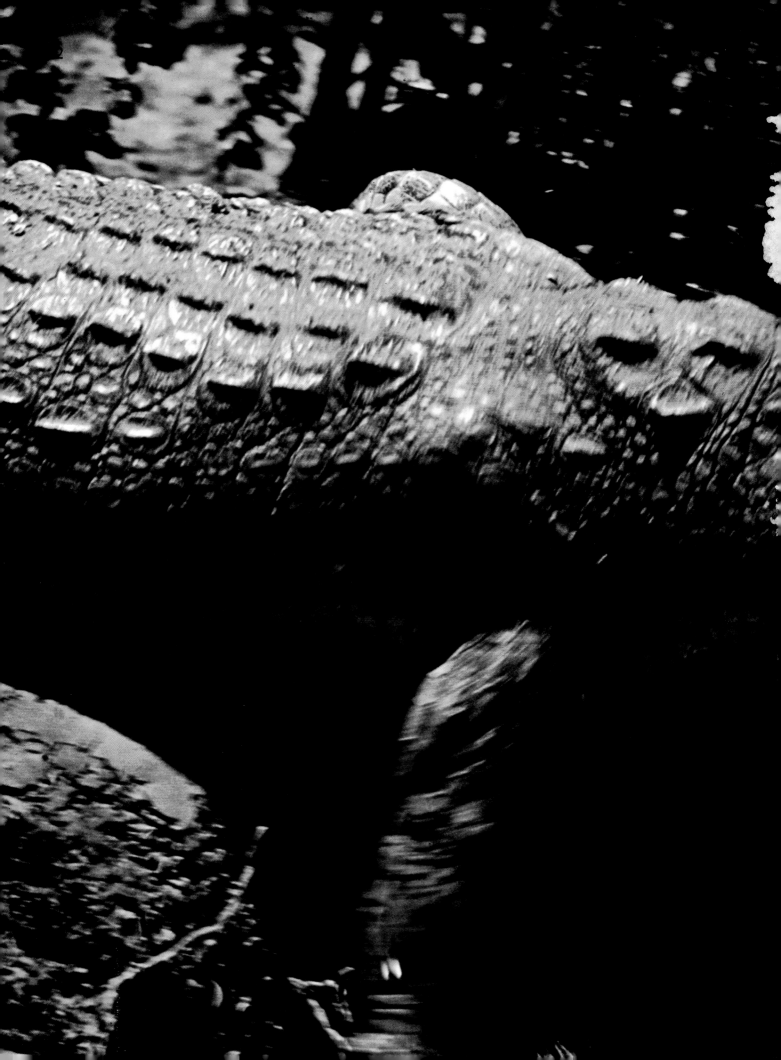

Baboons may not be very big, but they are strong, resourceful, and courageous. An attacking leopard would sooner retreat than battle a group of fierce 75-pound males. Several species of baboons occur in Africa. The animals live in troops, in which each individual's status is strictly defined. The troop is led by the strongest, most active males, who discipline and protect the others and decide the movements of the troop. An infant baboon is much admired by all the adults, and, by the fact of its birth, promotes its mother to the top of the troop's social scale. Grooming is a pastime that seems to bind the group together. The amount of grooming each baboon receives is decided by its status in the group. The dominant males, for example, get much more grooming than they give. Social status also determines the marching and fighting order. When traveling, females and infants with their bodyguard of dominant males remain at the center of the group, while the lower ranking males go before and behind. In case of attack, dominant males come to the front, while females and babies fall back. The troop observes certain natural boundaries in its wanderings which it never crosses. Sometimes the baboons fall in with other animals for mutual benefit, combining their sharp sight with the keen noses of other species. These primates are not good climbers, but they can run swiftly. They are moody animals with unpredictable tempers. They have been known to operate quite close to cities, even to enter and upset homes in the outlying areas. Man has no reason to hunt them unless they make pests of themselves.

Baboon munches
treetop delicacy.

Chimpanzees make ideal passengers for experimental flights into space. They are intelligent and biologically similar to man in many ways. But chimps are most at home high in the trees of the jungle forests. Their nests are sometimes 100 feet above the ground. Should an outsider pass beneath, the noisy band will protest its presence by making a terrific din of screams and hoots. Chimps are said to use tools, twigs that they shape especially for cleaning themselves and for grubbing bugs from trees. Now and then, chimps eat meat, but usually they are vegetarians. (In picture at right, a chimpanzee is tending a baby baboon.)

The innocent-looking vervets (overleaf) cause heavy damage to the crops of East African farmers. These monkeys live in groups of twenty to thirty or more, favoring heavily-wooded or bushy areas. They feed on vegetation and birds' eggs, are preyed upon by leopards and eagles.

Like most apes and monkeys,
vervet (below) and baboon are
affectionate mothers.

72

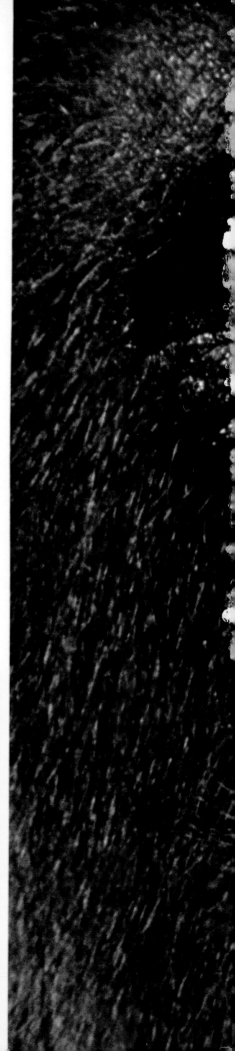

Gorillas look ferocious, but by nature they are gentle, peaceable vegetarians who live fairly undisturbed by man and the other animals. Only an occasional leopard has the daring to attack them. Gorillas live together in the African forests in groups of from six to seventeen. They are huge, powerful animals. A male stands 6 feet tall and weighs 600 pounds. Feeding occupies about eight hours of his day. The great beasts are too heavy to do much tree climbing, but the females and the young often sleep aloft, building a new nest each night. Each group has a leader, a male whose rule over the others is firm but fatherly. Females snuggle against this approachable chief and youngsters scramble over him in play. Gorillas shun civilization. Observers must seek them out deep in the African forests, even on the high slopes of the African mountains.

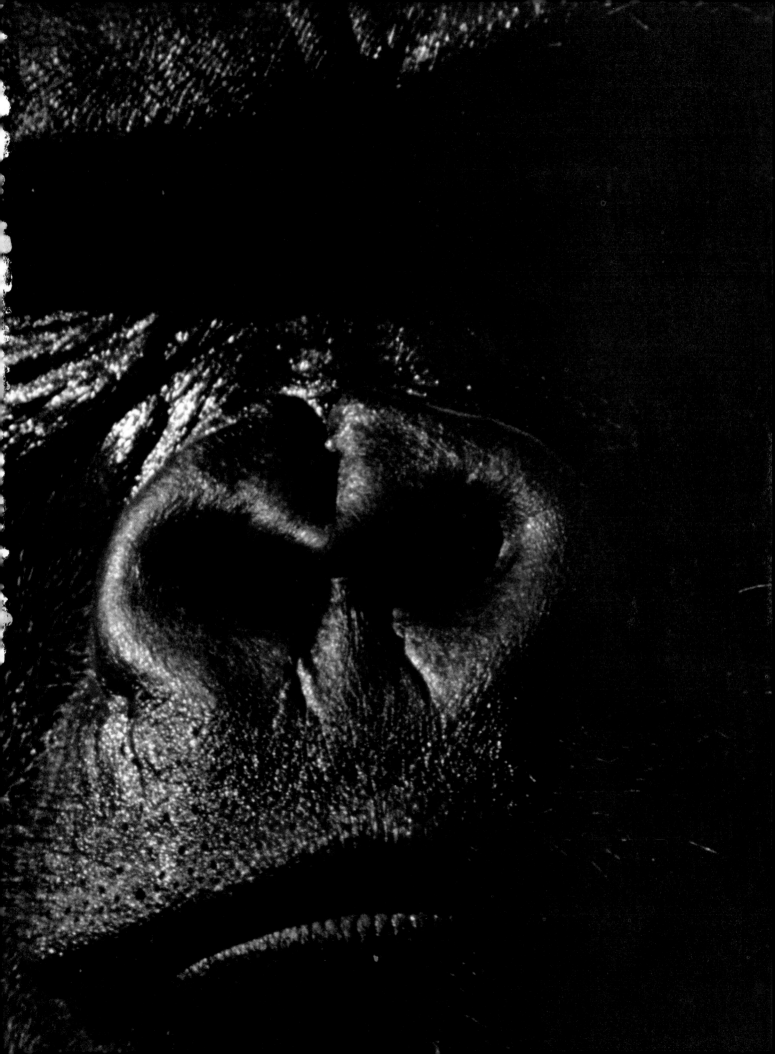

Hyenas are voracious scavengers of the African plain. After a lion or other predatory animal has finished feeding on its kill, hyenas, together with jackals and vultures in their turn, finish up the leavings. All but the largest bones of the largest animals can be cracked by the powerful jaws of the hyena. That is why no skeletons of dead animals are seen in areas where hyenas are plentiful. Besides disposing of carrion, hyenas do some hunting of their own, preying at night on newly-born and sickly animals. Man has little liking for the hyena, and no wonder. Its cry is unnerving, an eerie wail that rises from a hoarse growl to a high-pitched scream and often breaks into chuckles of hysterical "laughter." The hyena rarely attacks man, yet it readily eats the rubber tires off his trucks and airplanes. Likeable or not, the hyena fulfills a necessary function in nature, one that requires rapacity, strong jaws, and an even stronger stomach.

The scrappy little warthog, named for the large growths on the cheeks of the male, is the most common pig of the African plain. Left to itself, it snuffles about eating grass, fruit, and roots, dug up with its curved upper tusks. Home is a hole in the ground, often one vacated by an aardvark. Its fighting style is more comical than dangerous, for it rarely gets results from its furious threats and is rather easily put to rout. Warthogs are plentiful, and supply many a meal to the lion, leopard, cheetah, and wild dog.

Wild dogs, also known as hunting dogs, are among Africa's most fearsome and effective hunters. They work in packs, run their quarry to exhaustion, and tear it to pieces. Their usual victim is the Thomson's gazelle, impala, or other small-to-medium antelope. They hunt by sight, not scent, in the early morning and late afternoon. The pack leader selects the quarry and begins the pursuit. Two others trail him by a hundred yards to intercept the quarry if it should dodge or double back. The pack, numbering as many as forty, follows at a distance. Once begun, the hunt is almost always successful. The dogs are tireless and give up only if the prey crosses water. A wild dog pack is bound together so strongly that lone individuals of this species are almost unheard of. The pups are fed and raised attentively until they are old enough to leave their dens and join the pack. Wild dog packs occur sparsely and move from one hunting ground to another. While the number of kills that a pack makes is high, it stays in balance with the game levels.

O striches are birds that cannot fly. They are extremely shy, yet pack a punch powerful enough to disable even a horse. For good looks, the flamingo or even the stork would be preferred to the naked-necked, chicken-like ostrich, yet its black and white feathers were once so much the fad among fashionable women that in some parts of Africa the bird was hunted until there simply were no more. Being as much as 8 feet tall, an ostrich can't very easily hide itself, so it ducks its head down to the ground; it doesn't, as the saying goes, "bury its head in the sand." Except when defending its young, the ostrich prefers to run from danger. Why not? It can cover the ground in 25-foot strides and reach speeds up to 50 miles an hour. Ostriches are said to eat pebbles, and indeed they do. The stones help in the food-grinding function of the gizzard. But, of course, the ostriches wouldn't know that.